ISBN: 9798871587713
Imprint: Independently published

Cover design by: Art Painter
Library of Congress Control Number: 2018675309
Printed in the United States of America

"Amidst the celestial silence, our quest for extraterrestrial intelligence unfolds—a cosmic symphony awaiting the resonance of human curiosity. In the grand theater of the universe, let us listen for the echoes that transcend the boundaries of our cosmic existence and beckon us to decipher the messages written among the stars. For in the quiet expanse, the cosmic code whispers, and we, as cosmic listeners, stand on the threshold of revelations yet unseen."

CHIMEZIE IGWE

CONTENTS

PREFACE

Embarking on a Cosmic Odyssey

Welcome to the captivating exploration of the Science of Search for Extraterrestrial Intelligence (SETI). In the vast expanse of the cosmos, where stars twinkle like distant beacons and galaxies weave tales of cosmic wonders, our quest unfolds. This journey transcends the boundaries of scientific inquiry, venturing into the realms of human imagination, technological innovation, and the eternal fascination with the unknown.

As we turn our gaze to the stars, we delve into the rich tapestry of SETI's evolution—from the pioneering days of Project Ozma to the cutting-edge technologies of next-generation telescopes. Together, we navigate the theoretical landscapes of habitable zones, alternative biochemistries, and the enigmatic possibilities of extraterrestrial intelligence.

The cosmic conversation takes us beyond the traditional confines of radio signals, exploring the potential of optical communication and the search for distinctive technosignatures. We confront the challenges posed by the Fermi Paradox, grapple with the ethical considerations of Messaging Extraterrestrial Intelligence (METI), and witness the transformative role of artificial intelligence in our cosmic pursuits.

In this preface, we set the stage for an odyssey into the unknown, where interdisciplinary collaborations between astrophysics, astrobiology, and SETI redefine the contours of our cosmic understanding. The future beckons with promises of next-generation telescopes, sophisticated instruments, and the active engagement of a global community in the search for cosmic companionship.

Join us as we embark on this cosmic odyssey, where the silence of the cosmos beckons us to decipher the messages inscribed in the cosmic code. The quest for extraterrestrial intelligence becomes a shared journey, inviting everyone to be part of humanity's exploration into the vast expanse of the universe. Together, let us unravel the cosmic mysteries and embrace the wonders that await us among the stars.

INTRODUCTION
Unlocking the Cosmic Code - The Rich Tapestry of SETI Exploration

In the vast expanse of the cosmos, where stars shimmer like distant diamonds, humanity has embarked on a grand quest —to unravel the mysteries of the universe and, in particular, to seek out signs of extraterrestrial intelligence. This pursuit, encapsulated in the Science of Search for Extraterrestrial Intelligence (SETI), represents a captivating journey into the unknown, fueled by curiosity, technological innovation, and the enduring human spirit of exploration.

1.1 BACKGROUND OF SETI

In the annals of scientific inquiry, the origins of SETI trace back to a momentous idea articulated by the brilliant mind of physicist Enrico Fermi: "Where is everybody?" This poignant question, now famously known as the Fermi Paradox, encapsulates the seeming incongruity between the high probability of extraterrestrial civilizations in our galaxy and the conspicuous absence of evidence for their existence.

As we stand on the shoulders of scientific pioneers, the yearning to address Fermi's paradox led to the birth of SETI—a multidisciplinary field that amalgamates astronomy, astrobiology, and communication theory. Grounded in the idea that intelligent civilizations might communicate using electromagnetic signals, SETI's inception sparked a wave of enthusiasm to sift through the cosmic noise for potential messages from other sentient beings.

1.2 SIGNIFICANCE OF THE SEARCH FOR EXTRATERRESTRIAL INTELLIGENCE

The quest for extraterrestrial intelligence transcends the realm of scientific inquiry; it strikes at the heart of one of humanity's most profound questions: Are we alone in the universe? This existential query resonates across cultures and generations, binding us together in a shared fascination with the possibility of cosmic companionship.

Beyond the philosophical and existential dimensions, SETI carries profound implications for our understanding of life's potential ubiquity and diversity. The discovery of extraterrestrial intelligence would not only reshape our cosmic perspective but could also illuminate the vast tapestry of life's potential forms, perhaps as varied and intricate as the constellations that adorn our night sky.

1.3 HISTORICAL OVERVIEW OF SETI EFFORTS

The chronicles of SETI unfold against a backdrop of scientific ambition, technological progress, and the occasional flicker of tantalizing signals. In 1960, the pioneering astronomer Frank Drake conducted the first systematic search for extraterrestrial radio signals in what became known as Project Ozma. Pointing a radio telescope at two nearby stars, Tau Ceti and Epsilon Eridani, Drake's endeavor marked the inception of organized efforts to eavesdrop on cosmic conversations.

Since Project Ozma, SETI initiatives have evolved in tandem with technological advancements. The iconic Arecibo Observatory, with its colossal radio dish nestled in the Puerto Rican landscape, became a beacon of SETI research, scanning the skies for signals that might pierce through the cosmic veil. Over the years, the baton has passed to a new generation of telescopes and collaborative endeavors, each pushing the boundaries of our cosmic reach.

As we traverse the historical landscapes of SETI, we find ourselves at a juncture where the tools of inquiry are more potent than ever, where the interconnectedness of global scientific communities converges in a unified effort to decipher the enigmatic whispers of the cosmos.

In the ensuing chapters, we delve into the intricacies of the science of SETI, exploring the criteria for extraterrestrial life, the nuances of communication via radio signals, and the technological marvels propelling our quest. Join us as we navigate through the prominent projects, grapple with the challenges and controversies, and peer into the future, where artificial intelligence and evolving detection methods promise to reshape the very fabric of SETI exploration.

The cosmic code beckons, and humanity stands ready to decipher its messages—hoping, in the process, to uncover the profound secrets of our place in the cosmos.

THE SEARCH CRITERIA FOR EXTRATERRESTRIAL LIFE

2.1 CHARACTERISTICS OF HABITABLE ZONES

At the heart of the search for extraterrestrial intelligence lies the exploration of habitable zones—regions around stars where conditions may foster the emergence and sustenance of life. Our understanding of habitable zones has transcended the simplistic notion of a "Goldilocks zone," defined by a star's distance where liquid water can exist. Contemporary research seeks a nuanced understanding, considering factors such as stellar type, planetary composition, and atmospheric conditions.

Advancements in astrophysics have unveiled the diversity of potential habitable environments. Beyond Earth-like planets, exomoons and unconventional celestial bodies offer alternative abodes for life. These expanding horizons prompt us to reassess preconceived notions and broaden the scope of our search.

2.2 CONDITIONS FOR LIFE AS WE KNOW IT

Life on Earth serves as our only reference point, shaping our quest for extraterrestrial counterparts. The fundamental building blocks—carbon-based molecules, liquid water, and energy sources—establish a framework for identifying potentially habitable worlds. The study of extremophiles on Earth, organisms thriving in extreme environments, further broadens our definition of habitability and the conditions that may support life beyond our planet.

As our exploration extends to the far reaches of our solar system and beyond, the quest for life pushes the boundaries of our knowledge. The subsurface oceans of moons like Europa and Enceladus tantalize scientists with the prospect of life in unexpected locales, challenging traditional assumptions about habitability.

2.3 ALTERNATIVE BIOCHEMISTRIES AND LIFE FORMS

The pursuit of extraterrestrial life transcends the confines of Earth's biochemistry. While carbon-based life remains a focal point, scientific inquiry entertains the possibility of alternative biochemistries. Silicon-based life, for instance, presents a tantalizing prospect, with silicon sharing some chemical properties with carbon.

The exploration of exotic biochemistries extends to the very nature of life forms. Microbial life, multicellular organisms, or even intelligent, technologically advanced civilizations—all represent potential manifestations of extraterrestrial life. As we unravel the diverse tapestry of life on Earth, we open our minds to the myriad possibilities awaiting discovery among the stars.

In our ongoing pursuit of extraterrestrial intelligence, understanding the intricacies of habitable zones, the conditions conducive to life, and the diversity of potential biochemistries guides our search parameters. The cosmos, as a vast laboratory of possibilities, invites us to expand our horizons and redefine our preconceptions as we embark on the grand journey to uncover the secrets of life beyond Earth.

RADIO SIGNALS AS COMMUNICATION

3.1 THE BASIS FOR USING RADIO WAVES IN SETI

Central to the Science of Search for Extraterrestrial Intelligence (SETI) is the reliance on radio waves as a potential mode of communication between intelligent civilizations. The choice of radio signals is not arbitrary; it stems from the unique properties of radio waves that make them ideal for traversing the vast cosmic distances with relative ease. Unlike visible light, radio waves can penetrate interstellar dust clouds and endure minimal degradation over astronomical scales.

Within the electromagnetic spectrum, radio frequencies offer a wide bandwidth, allowing for the transmission of complex information. The practicality of using radio signals for communication is evident in our own technological evolution, from early radio broadcasts to modern satellite communications. Consequently, SETI researchers focus their efforts on scanning the cosmos for artificial radio signals that could indicate intentional attempts at cosmic conversation.

3.2 THE DRAKE EQUATION: ESTIMATING THE NUMBER OF COMMUNICATING CIVILIZATIONS

As we peer into the cosmic ocean, the Drake Equation serves as a conceptual compass, guiding our contemplation of the potential prevalence of extraterrestrial civilizations. Conceived by astronomer Frank Drake in 1961, the equation attempts to quantify the number of active, communicative extraterrestrial civilizations in our Milky Way galaxy.

$$N = R^* \times fp \times ne \times fl \times fi \times fc \times L$$

In this equation:

N: represents the number of civilizations with which humans could communicate.

R*: denotes the rate of star formation in our galaxy.

Fp: is the fraction of those stars that possess planetary systems.

ne: represents the number of planets within those systems capable of supporting life.

Fl: is the fraction of those planets where life actually evolves.

Fi: signifies the fraction of those planets where intelligent life develops.

Fc: represents the fraction of planets with intelligent life that develop technology for communication.

L: is the average lifespan of communicative civilizations.

While the Drake Equation offers a structured framework for discussion, its variables remain estimations, fueling ongoing debates within the scientific community about the likelihood of extraterrestrial intelligence.

3.3 CHALLENGES AND LIMITATIONS OF RADIO SIGNAL DETECTION

The quest to detect extraterrestrial radio signals encounters numerous challenges rooted in the vastness of space, the limitations of our technology, and the need to differentiate between natural and artificial sources. The cosmic distances between stars necessitate the use of highly sensitive instruments capable of discerning faint signals amidst the cacophony of cosmic noise.

Furthermore, distinguishing between signals of anthropogenic origin (i.e., human-made interference) and potential extraterrestrial signals requires sophisticated signal processing techniques. False positives and negatives loom as constant companions in the SETI endeavor, prompting researchers to continually refine detection methods and enhance the precision of their instruments.

In the chapters to come, we will delve deeper into the technological advances propelling the search for extraterrestrial intelligence, exploring not only radio signals but also the expanding array of methods and instruments that promise to unlock the secrets of the cosmos. The journey into the cosmos continues, guided by the persistent pulse of curiosity and the pursuit of answers to one of humanity's most profound questions

—Are we alone in the universe?

TECHNOLOGICAL ADVANCES IN SETI

4.1 RADIO TELESCOPE ARRAYS AND THEIR ROLE

At the forefront of the SETI quest are radio telescope arrays, colossal networks of interconnected radio antennas designed to capture and analyze celestial signals. The evolution from single-dish telescopes to sophisticated arrays represents a quantum leap in our ability to survey the cosmos comprehensively.

Notable among these arrays is the Very Large Array (VLA), a radio telescope facility in New Mexico comprising 27 individual antennas arranged in a Y-shaped configuration. The VLA, along with other global arrays, enables scientists to observe the sky with unprecedented resolution and sensitivity. By combining signals from multiple antennas, these arrays create a virtual telescope with dimensions equivalent to the separation between the antennas, enhancing our ability to detect weak signals and pinpoint their celestial origins.

4.2 OPTICAL SETI: SEARCHING FOR LASER SIGNALS

While radio waves dominate traditional SETI efforts, the exploration of extraterrestrial intelligence extends into the optical spectrum. Optical SETI, a complementary approach, focuses on detecting brief pulses of light or narrowband laser signals that could indicate intentional communication.

The advantages of optical SETI lie in the potential for higher data transfer rates and the ability to convey information using significantly less energy than traditional radio signals. Pioneering projects, such as the Breakthrough Listen Initiative's optical component, expand our observational toolkit, harnessing advancements in photonics and signal processing to scour the skies for elusive optical signals.

4.3 THE IMPACT OF ADVANCES IN SIGNAL PROCESSING

In the realm of SETI, the extraction of meaningful signals from the cosmic symphony relies heavily on sophisticated signal processing techniques. As computational capabilities burgeon, so does our ability to sift through vast datasets, identify potential signals, and discriminate between natural phenomena and artificial transmissions.

Machine learning algorithms, in particular, have emerged as invaluable tools in SETI research. These algorithms can analyze vast datasets in real-time, discerning patterns that may elude human observation. By training algorithms on known signals and noise, researchers aim to enhance the efficiency and accuracy of automated signal detection, reducing the likelihood of overlooking potential extraterrestrial communications.

The marriage of advanced signal processing techniques with cutting-edge telescope arrays marks a paradigm shift in SETI research. As we navigate the intricate dance of technology and theory, the cosmos reveals itself in ever-greater detail, beckoning us to decipher its secrets and unlock the mysteries of extraterrestrial intelligence.

In the ensuing chapters, we delve into the intricacies of prominent SETI projects, exploring the pivotal role these technological marvels play in our ongoing pursuit of cosmic companionship. Join us as we unravel the tapestry of technological innovation that propels humanity's quest to bridge the cosmic expanse and commune with potential extraterrestrial neighbors.

PROMINENT SETI PROJECTS AND INITIATIVES

5.1 PROJECT OZMA: THE FIRST ATTEMPT

The origins of SETI are eternally tied to Project Ozma, a pioneering endeavor that laid the groundwork for systematic searches for extraterrestrial intelligence. Conceived by astronomer Frank Drake in 1960, Project Ozma utilized the Green Bank Radio Telescope in West Virginia to observe two nearby stars, Tau Ceti and Epsilon Eridani, in the hopes of detecting artificial radio signals.

While Project Ozma did not yield definitive evidence of extraterrestrial signals, it marked a crucial milestone in the scientific exploration of the cosmos. It established the methodology for future SETI endeavors, emphasizing the importance of targeted observations and the need for continuous and systematic scans of the radio spectrum.

5.2 THE ARECIBO OBSERVATORY AND ITS CONTRIBUTIONS

No discussion of SETI would be complete without acknowledging the iconic Arecibo Observatory. Nestled in the Puerto Rican rainforest, the Arecibo dish, with its 305-meter diameter, held the title of the world's largest radio telescope for decades. Its unique design allowed for both radio astronomy and planetary radar observations, making it a versatile tool in the search for extraterrestrial intelligence.

Arecibo's contributions to SETI were monumental. Its sensitivity and ability to rapidly scan large portions of the sky made it a key player in numerous projects, including the SETI@home distributed computing initiative. Sadly, the Arecibo Observatory collapsed in 2020, marking the end of an era. However, its legacy endures in the lessons learned, the knowledge gained, and the inspiration it provided to subsequent generations of SETI researchers.

5.3 THE BREAKTHROUGH LISTEN INITIATIVE

In the contemporary landscape of SETI, the Breakthrough Listen Initiative stands as a beacon of ambition and collaboration. Launched in 2015 and backed by the Breakthrough Initiatives, this project leverages state-of-the-art telescopes, including the Green Bank Telescope and the Parkes Observatory, to survey the sky in unprecedented detail.

Breakthrough Listen adopts a multi-pronged approach, observing a wide range of frequencies and employing advanced signal processing techniques. Notably, it embraces optical SETI, expanding the search beyond radio waves to explore the possibility of laser signals. The initiative's commitment to open data access and collaboration with the global scientific community exemplifies a new era of transparency and shared discovery in the field.

5.4 OTHER INTERNATIONAL COLLABORATIONS IN SETI

As the quest for extraterrestrial intelligence transcends national boundaries, international collaborations have become instrumental in advancing SETI research. Organizations like the SETI Institute in the United States, the Square Kilometre Array (SKA) project involving multiple countries, and the European Space Agency's PLATO mission all contribute to the collective effort to decode potential cosmic messages.

The SKA, a mega-telescope project, promises unprecedented sensitivity and survey speed, ushering in a new era of radio astronomy and SETI. PLATO, designed to detect and characterize exoplanets, indirectly contributes to the search for extraterrestrial intelligence by identifying potentially habitable worlds where future SETI efforts could be focused.

As we traverse the landscape of prominent SETI projects, the collaborative spirit and technological prowess of the global scientific community become evident. Each project builds upon the lessons of its predecessors, pushing the boundaries of our cosmic gaze and bringing us one step closer to the elusive discovery of extraterrestrial intelligence.

In the forthcoming chapters, we navigate the intricacies of SETI's intersection with astrobiology, grapple with the ethical considerations of messaging extraterrestrial intelligence, and explore the role of public perception in shaping the discourse surrounding our search for cosmic companionship. The journey continues, propelled by the collective dreams and aspirations of humanity to uncover the cosmic secrets that lie beyond the celestial horizon.

SETI AND ASTROBIOLOGY

6.1 OVERLAPPING GOALS OF SETI AND ASTROBIOLOGY

SETI and astrobiology, seemingly distinct fields, share a common thread in their pursuit of understanding the potential for life beyond Earth. While astrobiology casts a wide net, encompassing the study of life's origin, evolution, and distribution in the universe, SETI hones in on the specific quest for intelligent extraterrestrial life and the potential for communication.

The intersection of these disciplines is evident in the quest for biosignatures—indicators of past or present life that may be detectable in the atmospheres of exoplanets. As SETI endeavors explore the cosmos for technosignatures (indications of advanced technological civilizations), astrobiological investigations seek clues that may reveal simpler forms of extraterrestrial life. The synergy between SETI and astrobiology amplifies the scope of our cosmic exploration, emphasizing the interconnectedness of the search for life in its myriad forms.

6.2 EXOPLANET DISCOVERIES AND THEIR IMPLICATIONS FOR SETI

The prolific discoveries of exoplanets, planets orbiting stars beyond our solar system, have revolutionized our understanding of the cosmos and injected newfound vigor into the quest for extraterrestrial intelligence. With thousands of exoplanets identified to date, including those within the habitable zone of their host stars, the tantalizing prospect of finding a celestial neighbor harboring life becomes increasingly plausible.

SETI benefits immensely from these discoveries, as each newfound exoplanet provides a potential target for further investigation. The identification of potentially habitable worlds fuels optimism, prompting SETI researchers to focus their efforts on regions of the galaxy where conditions may be conducive to the emergence of intelligent life. The synergy between exoplanet research and SETI underscores the symbiotic relationship between these fields, each informing and enriching the other in our shared quest for cosmic companions.

6.3 BIOSIGNATURES AND THE SEARCH FOR ALIEN LIFE

As astrobiologists scrutinize exoplanet atmospheres for biosignatures—indicators of life such as oxygen, methane, and other chemical imbalances—SETI researchers contemplate the potential technosignatures that advanced civilizations might produce. The search for biosignatures and technosignatures becomes a cosmic dialogue, where the presence of one may inform the likelihood of the other.

While biosignature detection aims to unveil the secrets of microbial or multicellular life, the identification of technosignatures could signify the presence of advanced extraterrestrial civilizations. The synergy between these pursuits underscores the holistic nature of our cosmic exploration, urging us to consider the interconnected web of possibilities that span the spectrum from microbial life to advanced intelligences capable of technological communication.

In the chapters ahead, we delve deeper into the challenges and controversies within the SETI landscape. As we navigate these intricacies, the intertwined nature of astrobiology and SETI becomes increasingly apparent, guiding our exploration of the cosmos with a multifaceted approach. The cosmic dialogue unfolds, transcending the boundaries of individual disciplines, as we strive to decode the messages that the universe might be waiting to share.

CHALLENGES AND CONTROVERSIES IN SETI

7.1 THE FERMI PARADOX: WHY HAVEN'T WE DETECTED EXTRATERRESTRIAL LIFE YET?

The persistent silence of the cosmos, devoid of any confirmed signals from extraterrestrial civilizations, gives rise to the perplexing Fermi Paradox. Named after physicist Enrico Fermi, the paradox encapsulates the apparent contradiction between the high probability of the existence of extraterrestrial civilizations and the lack of observable evidence for their presence.

Various hypotheses attempt to address the Fermi Paradox, ranging from the possibility that intelligent civilizations are rare, to the notion that they may self-destruct before reaching the capability for interstellar communication. The paradox fuels ongoing debates within the scientific community, prompting SETI researchers to continually refine their search strategies and reassess our assumptions about the prevalence of intelligent life in the cosmos.

7.2 ETHICAL CONSIDERATIONS IN MESSAGING EXTRATERRESTRIAL INTELLIGENCE (METI)

Amidst the fervent pursuit of listening for signals from extraterrestrial civilizations, another facet of the SETI endeavor raises ethical questions—Messaging Extraterrestrial Intelligence (METI). This involves intentionally sending signals from Earth with the aim of reaching potential extraterrestrial recipients.

Debates surrounding METI delve into the potential risks and benefits of actively broadcasting our presence to the cosmos. Critics argue that METI could attract the attention of potentially hostile extraterrestrial entities, while proponents view it as a means of initiating peaceful communication and collaboration. The ethical dimensions of METI add a layer of complexity to the already intricate landscape of SETI research, underscoring the need for careful consideration of our actions in the vast cosmic theater.

7.3 PUBLIC PERCEPTION AND THE MEDIA'S ROLE IN SHAPING SETI DISCOURSE

The public's perception of SETI is influenced not only by scientific discourse but also by media representation. Depictions of extraterrestrial life in popular culture, ranging from benevolent beings to menacing invaders, shape societal attitudes and expectations regarding SETI efforts.

Balancing the excitement of potential discovery with responsible communication is a delicate task. The media's portrayal of SETI initiatives can impact public support, funding, and even policy decisions. Striking a balance between fostering public enthusiasm for scientific exploration and avoiding sensationalism is crucial for maintaining a constructive and informed public discourse around the search for extraterrestrial intelligence.

As we navigate the complexities of the Fermi Paradox, grapple with the ethical considerations of METI, and assess the impact of media narratives on public perception, the landscape of SETI research becomes a dynamic interplay of scientific inquiry, philosophical contemplation, and societal engagement. In the chapters ahead, we explore the role of artificial intelligence in advancing SETI, examine the search for technosignatures, and peer into the future of this captivating scientific quest. The cosmos, seemingly silent, beckons us to unravel its mysteries, armed with both scientific rigor and a profound awareness of the broader implications of our cosmic inquiries.

THE ROLE OF ARTIFICIAL INTELLIGENCE IN SETI

8.1 MACHINE LEARNING AND DATA ANALYSIS IN SETI

In the evolving landscape of SETI research, the integration of artificial intelligence (AI) emerges as a transformative force. Machine learning algorithms, specifically designed for data analysis, are revolutionizing the way we sift through the immense volumes of information collected by radio telescope arrays.

Machine learning algorithms excel at recognizing patterns, a task particularly suited to the intricate and often subtle signals that SETI researchers seek. By training these algorithms on known signals and background noise, scientists can enhance the efficiency of signal detection, reducing the risk of false positives and ensuring a more targeted and accurate search for potential extraterrestrial communications.

The application of machine learning techniques extends beyond signal detection. In data preprocessing, noise reduction, and signal classification, AI-driven approaches promise to streamline and optimize the entire SETI workflow, opening new frontiers in our ability to unravel the cosmic code.

8.2 AUTOMATED DETECTION SYSTEMS AND ALGORITHMS

The adoption of automated detection systems represents a natural evolution in SETI methodology. These systems, guided by sophisticated algorithms, can autonomously process vast datasets in real-time, significantly augmenting the speed and efficiency of the search for extraterrestrial signals.

Prominent among these systems is the Breakthrough Listen Initiative's automated signal detection pipeline. This cutting-edge tool operates on the colossal datasets generated by radio telescopes, employing advanced algorithms to identify potential signals worthy of closer scrutiny. The integration of automated detection systems not only accelerates the pace of analysis but also allows researchers to focus their efforts on the most promising candidates, maximizing the chances of discovering meaningful extraterrestrial communications.

8.3 FUTURE PROSPECTS OF AI IN ADVANCING SETI RESEARCH

As AI continues to advance, the future of SETI research appears increasingly intertwined with the capabilities of intelligent algorithms. Predictive modeling, neural networks, and unsupervised learning methods offer untapped potential for unlocking subtle patterns in the cosmic signalscape.

The integration of AI extends beyond signal processing. Machine learning algorithms can assist in the interpretation of complex data, aiding researchers in discerning potential technosignatures from natural phenomena. The synergy between human expertise and artificial intelligence augurs a future where SETI research becomes not only more efficient but also more insightful, pushing the boundaries of our understanding of the cosmos.

In the forthcoming chapters, we explore the implications of these technological advancements on the search for technosignatures, as well as the ethical considerations surrounding the use of artificial intelligence in our quest to decode potential messages from extraterrestrial civilizations. The marriage of human ingenuity and machine intelligence promises to shape the next chapter in the ongoing saga of SETI exploration, inviting us to envision a future where the cosmic code is deciphered with unprecedented precision and efficiency.

SETI AND THE SEARCH FOR TECHNOSIGNATURES

9.1 TECHNOLOGICAL ARTIFACTS AS SIGNS OF ADVANCED CIVILIZATIONS

In the expansive search for extraterrestrial intelligence, the quest for technosignatures takes center stage. Unlike traditional biosignatures that indicate the presence of life, technosignatures point to the existence of advanced technological civilizations. The search for these signals, artifacts, or anomalies represents a shift in focus from merely detecting signs of life to identifying the fingerprints of intelligent, technologically adept beings.

Theoretical technosignatures encompass a wide array of possibilities, including large-scale engineering projects, megastructures, or even the inadvertent consequences of industrial activity. Dyson Spheres, hypothetical structures encompassing entire stars to harness their energy, represent one captivating example of a potential technosignature. The search for these distinctive markers requires a combination of innovative technologies, sophisticated data analysis, and a keen understanding of the possible manifestations of advanced civilizations.

9.2 DYSON SPHERES AND OTHER TECHNOLOGICAL MEGASTRUCTURES

The concept of Dyson Spheres, popularized by British-American science fiction writer Olaf Stapledon and later by British-American science fiction writer and biochemist Sir Arthur C. Clarke, imagines an advanced civilization harnessing the energy of its host star. While the practicality of constructing such megastructures remains speculative, the idea captures the imagination of SETI researchers as they consider the potential visibility of these colossal feats of engineering.

Beyond Dyson Spheres, other technological megastructures, such as Alderson Disks or Niven Rings, represent additional avenues for technosignature exploration. These hypothetical constructs, if realized by advanced civilizations, could leave observable imprints on the cosmic stage, providing tantalizing targets for SETI investigations.

9.3 LIMITS AND CHALLENGES IN TECHNOSIGNATURE DETECTION

The search for technosignatures encounters significant challenges rooted in the vastness of space, the limitations of current technology, and the unpredictability of extraterrestrial civilizations. The sheer distance between stars necessitates the use of advanced telescopes capable of discerning minute details across interstellar expanses. Additionally, distinguishing between natural celestial phenomena and potential technosignatures requires meticulous scrutiny and robust methodologies.

The limits of our current technological capabilities pose another obstacle. The detection of subtle signals or anomalies amidst the cosmic noise demands increasingly sensitive instruments and innovative data analysis techniques. Moreover, the assumption that extraterrestrial civilizations would utilize technology comparable to our own introduces an anthropocentric bias that may hinder our ability to recognize truly novel or exotic technosignatures.

In the chapters ahead, we delve into the cutting-edge technologies and methodologies employed in the search for technosignatures, exploring the collaborative efforts of international initiatives and the ongoing advancements that propel us closer to unraveling the mysteries of potential cosmic neighbors. The pursuit of technosignatures expands the horizons of SETI, challenging us to envision the vast array of possibilities that the cosmos holds for the manifestation of intelligent, technologically advanced life.

FUTURE DIRECTIONS AND PROSPECTS

10.1 NEXT-GENERATION TELESCOPES AND INSTRUMENTS

The future of the Search for Extraterrestrial Intelligence (SETI) is intricately tied to the development of next-generation telescopes and instruments. Advancements in observational capabilities promise to revolutionize our ability to survey the cosmos for potential signals and technosignatures.

Projects such as the Square Kilometre Array (SKA) and the James Webb Space Telescope (JWST) exemplify the cutting-edge technologies that will soon come online. The SKA, a colossal radio telescope array, aims to be the most powerful radio telescope ever constructed, offering unprecedented sensitivity and survey speed. Simultaneously, the JWST, set to launch into space, will enable observations in the infrared spectrum, providing new insights into distant exoplanets and their atmospheres.

The synergy between these and other upcoming instruments amplifies the scope of our cosmic gaze, bringing us closer to the realization of a comprehensive and systematic search for extraterrestrial intelligence. As these telescopes come online, the data they generate will fuel an era of discovery, marking a pivotal moment in our quest to uncover the cosmic secrets.

10.2 INTERDISCIPLINARY COLLABORATIONS WITH ASTROPHYSICS AND ASTROBIOLOGY

The frontiers of SETI are expanding through interdisciplinary collaborations that bridge the realms of astrophysics and astrobiology. The collaboration between these fields enhances our understanding of the conditions conducive to life and the potential habitats that might host extraterrestrial intelligence.

Astrophysical discoveries, such as the identification of exoplanets within habitable zones, provide valuable targets for SETI investigations. Conversely, SETI research informs astrobiology by delving into the potential technosignatures that may accompany the emergence of advanced civilizations. The symbiotic relationship between these disciplines reinforces the holistic approach required for unraveling the cosmic code.

10.3 PUBLIC ENGAGEMENT AND THE FUTURE OF CITIZEN SCIENCE IN SETI

Public engagement is a cornerstone of the future of SETI, as the quest for extraterrestrial intelligence captures the collective imagination of humanity. Initiatives like SETI@home, which harness the computational power of volunteers worldwide, represent a model for citizen science involvement. By involving the public in the analysis of radio signals, SETI@home not only accelerates data processing but also fosters a sense of shared responsibility and excitement in the pursuit of cosmic discovery.

Future endeavors may further capitalize on the enthusiasm of citizen scientists, engaging them in the search for technosignatures, analysis of astronomical data, and even the formulation of research questions. The democratization of scientific inquiry through citizen science initiatives promises to redefine the relationship between scientists and the public, turning the search for extraterrestrial intelligence into a collaborative and inclusive endeavor.

In the final chapters of our exploration, we contemplate the ever-evolving landscape of SETI research. We peer into the horizon of possibilities shaped by advanced technologies, interdisciplinary collaborations, and the active participation of a global community. The cosmic symphony plays on, and as humanity takes its place among the stars, the quest to uncover the secrets of the universe becomes a shared journey, inviting everyone to be a part of the cosmic conversation.

CONCLUSION
Deciphering the Cosmic Code

As we conclude our expedition into the Science of Search for Extraterrestrial Intelligence (SETI), we find ourselves at the nexus of scientific curiosity, technological innovation, and the eternal human quest for understanding. The journey through the rich tapestry of SETI has unfolded across the epochs, from the pioneering days of Project Ozma to the cutting-edge technologies of next-generation telescopes, from the contemplation of biosignatures to the exploration of enigmatic technosignatures.

The cosmic code, inscribed in the electromagnetic signals that traverse the vastness of space, remains elusive but not beyond reach. Our exploration has traversed the theoretical landscapes of habitable zones and alternative biochemistries, delved into the intricacies of radio signals and the potential of optical communication, and grappled with the challenges posed by the Fermi Paradox and the ethical considerations of Messaging Extraterrestrial Intelligence (METI).

Technological marvels, such as AI-driven algorithms and automated detection systems, stand as sentinels at the forefront of our cosmic inquiry, promising to unveil patterns and anomalies that may reveal the presence of intelligent extraterrestrial life. The collaboration between disciplines—astrobiology, astrophysics, and SETI—harmonizes our cosmic exploration, weaving together a narrative that transcends individual boundaries of expertise.

As we gaze into the future, the cosmic conversation

expands its horizons. Next-generation telescopes and instruments beckon us to explore the cosmos with unprecedented precision, offering glimpses into distant worlds and potential signals that may echo across the light-years. Interdisciplinary collaborations sculpt a nuanced understanding of the conditions necessary for life and the potential pathways that lead to the emergence of intelligent civilizations.

Public engagement becomes not only a reflection of humanity's collective fascination with the cosmos but a vital force propelling the SETI endeavor forward. Citizen scientists, equipped with passion and computational power, contribute to the ongoing search, transforming it into a shared exploration that knows no geographical or disciplinary boundaries.

As we stand on the precipice of the unknown, the cosmic code calls out to us, inviting us to decipher its messages and unlock the profound secrets of the universe. The search for extraterrestrial intelligence is a quest that extends beyond the boundaries of science; it is a journey that kindles the human spirit, fosters collaboration, and fuels the imagination of generations yet unborn.

In the grand cosmic theater, where stars twinkle like distant beacons and galaxies paint the canvas of the night sky, humanity plays the role of the cosmic listener. The silence may persist, the signals may remain elusive, but as we continue to probe the cosmic depths, our yearning for cosmic companionship remains undiminished. The cosmic code, inscribed in the whispers of the cosmos, remains an open book, inviting us to turn its pages and explore the infinite possibilities that await us among the stars. The quest for extraterrestrial intelligence, with its uncertainties and triumphs, embodies the indomitable spirit of human exploration—a spirit that propels us ever onward, into the cosmic unknown.

www.ingramcontent.com/pod-product-compliance
Lightning Source LLC
Chambersburg PA
CBHW060212260726
48658CB00005BA/2009